B 1

CROFTING AND THE ENVIRONMENT:
A NEW APPROACH

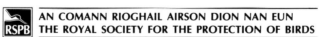

AN COMANN RIOGHAIL AIRSON DION NAN EUN
THE ROYAL SOCIETY FOR THE PROTECTION OF BIRDS

The Scottish Crofters Union
Old Mill, Broadford, Isle of Skye, Inverness-shire, IV49 9AQ.
and
The Royal Society for the Protection of Birds
Scottish Headquarters, 17 Regent Terrace, Edinburgh, EH7 5BN.

This document was prepared by a project team led by Dr Tim Stowe, North Scotland Regional Officer of the RSPB,
and George Campbell, Director of the SCU.

Front Cover photographs; Machair on Barra, Hugh Webster; Corncrake, C H Gomersall/RSPB; Turning hay, HIE.

The publishers acknowledge permission to reproduce photographs by;

John Charity, Dennis Coutts, Eòlas (Sam Maynard), C H Gomersall/RSPB, HIE,
Cailean Maclean, Murdo Macleod, M W Richards/RSPB, RSPB, T J Stowe, Charles Tait,
Hugh Webster, D S Whitaker/NCCS

Published by The Royal Society for the Protection of Birds and The Scottish Crofters Union 1992.
© The Royal Society for the Protection of Birds and The Scottish Crofters Union 1992.
All rights reserved. No part of this publication may be reproduced without the prior permission of
The Royal Society for the Protection of Birds and The Scottish Crofters Union.
Designed and typeset by Acair Ltd, Stornoway, Isle of Lewis.
Printed by Highland Printers, Inverness.

ISBN 0 90313 849

CROFTING AND THE ENVIRONMENT: A NEW APPROACH

Acknowledgements

In the first instance, we wish to express our gratitude to Highland Regional Council and Highlands and Islands Enterprise for their financial assistance towards this project.

During the course of our research, many people have contributed their time and individual skills towards the realisation of this document. Our thanks are due primarily to the staff of our two organisations, The Scottish Crofters Union and The Royal Society for the Protection of Birds, and to the crofters who took the time to participate in our interviews. We also wish to express our thanks to everyone who submitted photographs for selection, and to the organisations noted below, for providing information and advice.

Acair Publishing Limited
Caithness and Sutherland Local Enterprise Company
Crofters Commission
Highland Fund Limited
Highland Regional Council
Highlands and Islands Enterprise
Highlands and Islands Livestock Limited
Lewis Livestock Limited
Nature Conservancy Council for Scotland
Orkney Islands Council
Red Deer Commission
Scottish Agricultural Colleges
Scottish Office Agriculture and Fisheries Department
Shetland Islands Council
Shetland Lamb Marketing Cooperative Limited
Strathclyde Regional Council
Western Isles Islands Council

The project team consisted of:
Lloyd Austin, Conservation Planning Officer (Scotland), RSPB
George Campbell, Director, SCU
Janet Egdell, Rural Economist, RSPB
Sine Gillespie, Project Officer
Dr James Hunter, Author/Journalist/former Director of SCU
Dr Tim Stowe, North Scotland Regional Officer, RSPB
with the guidance of:
Neil Black, Senior Planner, Highland Regional Council
Dr. John Taylor, Head of Policy Research, RSPB
Melvyn Waumsley, Head of Environmental Policy, Highlands and Islands Enterprise

Murdo McLeod

Hay drying, Isle of Lewis

CONTENTS

FOREWORD

The crofting counties of Scotland have long been noted for their outstanding natural environment. Highland and Island landscapes are among the most spectacular in Europe. The unpolluted countryside supports a wide range of wildlife, including many rare habitats and species. In Britain, for instance, the corncrake, a globally threatened bird, has become almost synonymous with crofting.

This environment is, in part, a product of crofting practices. Many traditional aspects of crofting land-use, and thus the rich environment, have been maintained while the countryside elsewhere in the UK has witnessed great changes.

Crofting traditions also help to sustain distinct cultures. Many crofting areas retain relatively high human populations and thriving communities. These cultures, the community spirit and the diversified rural economy can also be related to the nature of crofting with its small, part-time holdings.

Nevertheless, not all is well with crofting. In this document, we consider changes in land-use practices which are affecting the environment and may threaten the nature of the crofting communities. In places, these changes have historically led to conflict between crofters and conservationists. We look beyond this conflict and examine why crofters are changing their land management. We go on to explore ideas that may help secure the future of the crofting environment and traditions, while sustaining a fair standard of living for crofters.

In what we believe to be a unique collaboration, The Scottish Crofters Union and The Royal Society for the Protection of Birds have come together to publish these proposals for a new approach to crofting. The ideas put forward here have been developed by a joint working group of representatives from each organisation. The group has also consulted a wide range of interested parties, including a number of working crofters.

A complete solution is beyond the scope of this paper, but our specific recommendations would make an important contribution. In developing these ideas further, we believe our underlying principles are sound. These are that future rural policy must combine social, agricultural and environmental objectives, that agriculture should be sustainable and that crofters and other landusers should be rewarded for sound management of the countryside, not simply food production.

With CAP reform firmly on the European agenda, this paper makes a timely contribution to the debate: we hope our ideas receive widespread support - from individual crofter to EC Commissioner. The SCU and RSPB look forward to future collaboration with others to further these proposals and achieve a secure future for crofters and the natural environment.

Iain MacIver
President, SCU.

Barbara S Young
Chief Executive ,RSPB.

Eòlas

Traditional cropping maintains a mosaic of land uses

SUMMARY AND RECOMMENDATIONS

Crofting is the small-scale, part-time traditional land use found in the Highlands and Islands of Scotland. It has created and maintained a rich and varied natural environment, as well as retaining thriving communities, with a high population density in some of the most remote areas of Britain. The Scottish Crofters Union and The Royal Society for the Protection of Birds, seek a secure future for crofting and its natural environment. In this joint initiative, we paint a picture of crofting in the future and give ideas for achieving this vision.

The history of crofting has been one of struggle to survive despite natural and man-made disadvantages; this is still very much the situation today, as shown in Chapter 1, *The Case for Crofting*. Agricultural and rural policies, which have considerable influence on crofting, are undergoing a process of radical change within Europe. We hope that crofting will emerge from the current period of uncertainty and readjustment in a stronger and more secure position.

Chapter 2, *Crofting in 2010*, outlines a future for crofting that benefits both crofters and their environment. In the future, crofting should be rewarded for the public goods it provides. We hope to see a greater proportion of croft land in active occupancy, more young people involved in crofting and more employment opportunities off the croft, with greater flexibility to accommodate work on the croft. We would like to see more diversification of croft land use, with less dependence on sheep. An increase in the ratio of cattle to sheep would add to the diversity of vegetation because of their different grazing habits, and a reduction in sheep numbers on much of the moorland and heathland would enhance its conservation interest. Regional forestry strategies would direct new planting to the areas of least wildlife value. There should be a greater area of late-cut silage and hay, to increase the extent of meadows for the globally threatened corncrake, together with the use of cutting methods that avoid destroying nests and killing birds. We would also envisage greater areas of crops, partly to increase crofters' self-sufficiency and partly to provide a range of habitats for wildlife.

In Chapter 3, *Supporting Crofting*, we suggest how this future could be attained, through the adjustment of the current support system for crofting. We recommend that:

1.   A new support system for crofting should be introduced, using cross compliance as the mechanism for linking all the schemes available to crofters to the provision of environmental benefits.

2. Within the regional zones proposed by the EC to accompany CAP reform, the UK government should insist that there is some degree of prioritisation, with the crofting region given the highest priority.

3. A co-ordinating agency should be identified, to act as the contact for crofters in respect of all schemes.

4. SOAFD should improve the existing Environmentally Sensitive Area (Machair of the Uists and Benbecula, Barra and Vatersay ESA), extend ESA agreements to at least 10 years and designate other substantial parts of the crofting counties as ESAs, with the aim that all crofters become eligible for such a scheme.

5. A premium for late-cut silage and hay should be introduced. This could initially be run by SNH as a Corncrake Grant Scheme (similar to that in Northern Ireland), but in the long-term the coordinating agency should manage the premium as part of the overall environmentally sensitive farming scheme.

6. The Marginal Cropping Grant should be reintroduced.

7. Livestock subsidies should be converted from a headage to a hectarage basis.

8. Townships should draw up conservation plans, detailing management of grazing, woodlands and access, and, in return, be entitled to woodland grants, communal management premia and concessions on freight costs.

9. Grazing committees should be given the power to enforce these conservation plans where they relate to common grazings.

10. The UK government should introduce direct income aids for crofters over 55 years old who are not working their croft and who agree to assign it to a new would-be crofter.

11. Overall, therefore, the financial support for crofting should be increased in recognition of the public goods and services provided by crofters.

This document shows how significant crofting is, in both social and environmental terms. In Chapter 4, *The Way Forward*, we emphasise how important it is that all the organisations involved with or having an impact on crofting are aware of this significance. We see this document as a catalyst, initiating further discussion on the ways in which crofting support and crofting administration can be reformed, so that crofting communities and their natural environment can look forward to a better future.

C H Gomersall/RSPB

Tall vegetation provides important early season cover for corncrakes

Charles Tait

The decline in cattle numbers has contributed to a poorer environment

CHAPTER ONE

THE CASE FOR CROFTING

1.1

In both the United Kingdom and the wider European Community agricultural and rural policy is currently undergoing far-reaching reassessment. Crofting cannot be isolated from this process. Adjustments in agricultural support mechanisms, for example, have helped bring about the recent and very steep decline in returns to crofting area sheep producers. Further such impacts are widely anticipated. That is why crofters, like the rest of the agricultural community, feel extremely insecure about their future.

1.2

The fundamental policy changes now taking place, however, need not be wholly negative from a crofting point of view. Indeed it is possible to envisage - as this document certainly envisages - crofting eventually emerging from the current period of readjustment in much stronger shape than ever before. But no such overall betterment in crofting conditions will occur automatically. It will come about only as a result of crofters and their representatives engaging forcefully, energetically and constructively in the growing public and political debate about the British and European rural future. This paper is intended to stimulate such engagement.

1.3

In one important respect, this document's publication is itself evidence of a new departure in crofting affairs. It marks the first major collaboration between a crofting group, The Scottish Crofters Union, and a conservation organisation, The Royal Society for the Protection of Birds. The paper's authors readily acknowledge that crofters and conservationists have not always seen eye to eye in the past. They recognise that future disagreement cannot be ruled out. But the contributors to this paper are equally convinced that both crofting and environmental interests can be well served by joint ventures of the type which have resulted in this paper's appearance. Figure 1.1 shows that the crofting counties have the largest number of species of notable breeding birds in the United Kingdom, illustrating how the interests of our two organisations coincide.

1.4

This document aims to show the importance of maintaining and enhancing crofting. It suggests how the organisations involved can take steps towards ensuring a secure future for crofters and their environment. In this sense, and in several others, this document is best regarded as a starting point. Much more will have to be done in order to finalise policies for crofting and for the quite outstanding natural environment with which crofting is associated. Both the British Government and the European Commission need to be convinced of crofting's merits. Crofters themselves will require to think seriously about what it is that they want to get out of the quickly changing circumstances in which they find themselves.

Crofting's Natural Environment

Scotland's crofting areas are associated with one of the world's most outstanding natural environments. The Highlands and Islands are scenically magnificent. They are immensely varied geologically and contain some of our planet's oldest rocks and fossils. While woodland cover has been much reduced in recent centuries, the region contains many woodland fragments where native tree species - such as birch, oak, ash and Scots pine - still flourish. The Highlands and Islands are dominated by their hills and uplands. But the region also contains coastal grasslands, a great deal of moorland and some of the most extensive blanket bogs and peatlands in the world. These various habitats are associated with animals such as the otter, the wildcat and the pine marten - as well as with significant populations of breeding birds such as golden eagle, corncrake, dunlin, whimbrel and greenshank. The Highlands and Islands are surrounded by some of our planet's richest seas, the waters around the crofting areas supporting an immense diversity of marine life as well as internationally important populations of seabirds. Their endlessly varied landscapes and exceptionally rich natural environment make the crofting areas important nationally and internationally. These features, together with the extent to which they have been conserved and safeguarded by crofting land use, give crofting communities a strong claim on the financial resources now beginning to be directed towards more environmentally sensitive types of agricultural support.

Crofting supports densely populated rural communities

Crofting sustains diverse, low intensity land management

1.9

Further reforms followed. In the first quarter of the present century, for instance, large tracts of the land which had previously been lost to crofters were brought back into crofting tenure by means of an extensive programme of state sponsored land settlement.

1.10

But for all these gains, crofting communities continued to be economically depressed. Crofts - even the new crofts created on those land settlement estates which were bought by early twentieth century public agencies - remained small. Crofters depended as much as ever on non-agricultural income. All too often, little or no such income was available. The inevitable outcome was continuing depopulation - the rate of outflow being such as to deprive many crofting localities of as much as a quarter or a third of all their people in the period between the 1920s and the 1950s.

1.11

After 1886 no government was willing to contemplate crofting's complete disappearance - not least because of a widespread public conviction that the crofting areas were deserving of a better deal. Crofter housing conditions were improved by the introduction of continuing grant and loan schemes. Crofters became eligible for a share of the extraordinarily generous agricultural support payments made available to the wider

---

Crofting Communities

For all that they have experienced a good deal of depopulation over the last hundred or so years, crofting communities are still much more densely populated than comparable areas elsewhere. This is because crofts are so much smaller than farms. A piece of land which, if it were in another part of Britain, might contain one or two farms can readily provide several dozen crofts. That is why some of the crofting communities in the Western Isles, for example, are more densely populated than any other rural locality in Britain outside the suburban south of England. Because they manage their land at a low intensity, however, these crofting communities co-exist with some of Britain's most valuable natural habitats.

---

farming industry in the years immediately following the Second World War. But no such assistance, by itself, was capable of reversing the now endemic decline of crofting.

1.12

This was partly because of a fundamental incompatibility between the wider objectives of UK and EC farming policy and the highly specific needs of crofting areas.

1.13

Both UK governments and the European Commission were committed, until the 1980s, to agricultural support systems geared to the production of more and more food. Hence the extent to which public money was deployed in such a way as to provide financial incentives to mechanise, intensify and amalgamate farms. Such measures could not be applied fully in a crofting context, however, without removing the security of tenure and other provisions of the 1886 Crofters Act and subsequent legislation. Although at the time the Agricultural Department for Scotland advocated just such drastic action, it was ultimately thought to be safer politically to permit crofting to retain its unique legislative status. Indeed that status was further enhanced in 1955 with the passing of a new Crofters Act and the establishment of the modern Crofters Commission.

1.14

The Commission's founding legislation made it responsible for the regulation of crofting by empowering it to supervise a wide range of tenancy transfers and matters of that kind. The Commission was also given the job of promoting the economic development of crofting communities. The developmental tools available to the Commission, however, consisted solely of the package of agricultural aids known as the Crofting Counties Agricultural Grants (Scotland) Scheme (CCAGS). Much was achieved by means of

CCAGS. However the scheme was purely agricultural in orientation - something which reflected both the national preconceptions of the 1950s and officialdom's more longstanding failure to come properly to grips with the implications of the part-time nature of farming throughout the crofting areas. The Crofters Commission did not therefore have the capacity to engage meaningfully in the overall regeneration of the crofting economy.

1.15

Increasingly, therefore, the Commission has contented itself with its regulatory role and with the administration of CCAGS - which has long since become simply one more set of standardised cash grants. The formulation of new strategies and initiatives designed to enhance crofting prospects by expanding the range both of agricultural and non-agricultural opportunities available to crofters and their families has been left to others - most notably the Highlands and Islands Development Board (HIDB) and its successor body, Highlands and Islands Enterprise (HIE), together with HIE's associated network of Local Enterprise Companies (LECs).

1.16

The present rethinking of rural policy offers crofting an important opportunity to rationalise and streamline the crofting administrative structure. This has become immensely complicated, legalistic, top-heavy and bureaucratic.

Confusion and Complexity in Crofting Regulations

Each of the many attempts to grapple with crofting difficulties has left its own institutional residue. The fixing of fair rents for crofts - by means of procedures laid down in 1886 - is a matter for the Scottish Land Court. The estates acquired for land settlement purposes in the 1920s are administered by the Scottish Office Agriculture and Fisheries Department (SOAFD) which also takes care of the crofter housing scheme. The Crofters Commission administers the Crofting Counties Agricultural Grants (Scotland) Scheme (CCAGS) and oversees the plethora of rules and regulations stemming from the Crofting Acts of 1955, 1961 and 1976. Both Highlands and Islands Enterprise and the various Local Enterprise Companies have their own crofting involvements. The European Commission takes a close interest in rural development in crofting areas. United Kingdom and European Community agricultural support payments of the kind which are available both to farmers and crofters are disbursed by SOAFD. Further complexities arise from the crofting interests of, among others, Scottish Natural Heritage, the Red Deer Commission and the many local authorities. The case for some degree of rationalisation is made stronger by the fact that crofting measures dating from one epoch are sometimes in conflict with different measures from another period. CCAGS assistance, administered by the Crofters Commission and introduced in the 1950s, can be utilised only for strictly agricultural purposes. Other aid available under the terms of the more recently introduced Rural Enterprise Programme, administered by SOAFD and HIE, can be spent only on projects which are strictly non-agricultural. This is all the more nonsensical in that both schemes are regularly made available to the same crofters by the same officials.

1.17

A still more exciting opportunity is offered by the fact that the changing objectives of both UK and EC policy for the countryside are making it possible to devise altogether new approaches to crofting. These approaches, a number of which are suggested in this paper, would give a much higher national priority than previously to the maintenance - and indeed expansion - of the crofting structure and the various land use patterns with which that structure is associated.

1.18

Crofting legislation is highly defensive in character. This is understandable in that much of it was introduced to safeguard crofting from forces which would otherwise have overwhelmed it. Thus the Act of 1886 gave crofters protection - by means of its security of tenure and rent-control provisions - from exploitative landlords. The Act of 1955 was similarly designed to shield the crofting structure from these commercial and political pressures which were then resulting in the marked trend towards much larger, more intensively managed, agricultural units in the rest of the United Kingdom.

1.19

Such an approach was necessary in the past. It is arguably less necessary today in that the major changes now occurring in the nature of agricultural and rural policies are resulting in these policies becoming, in principle at least, much more favourable to the continuation of crofting.

1.20

When the UK and European countryside was viewed primarily in terms of its food production potential, the case for crofting was undoubtedly weak - in that the part-time and low input character of crofting agriculture did not lend itself to yield enhancement of the sort which policy-makers were demanding. But now that both the UK government and the European Commission are placing more and more stress on the need to create a more diversified rural economy and a more environmentally attractive countryside, the case for crofting has been totally transformed. The crofting areas had comparatively little to offer nationally and internationally in food production terms. As a model of how rural communities can be organised in ways which both safeguard the natural environment and permit the integration of agriculture with a wide range of other income-earning activities, however, the crofting experience is of quite outstanding importance.

1.21

It is this paper's basic contention that the significance of crofting should be explicitly recognised both by the UK government and by the European Community. This will require a complete overturning of previous attitudes. Instead of crofting being regarded as some sort of quaint anachronism, possibly deserving of preservation in much the same way as a thatched cottage or a medieval mill, crofting ought now to be seen as a first-rate means to achieving policy objectives of the type now being proposed right across the EC.

Crofting and Wildlife in Shetland

In Shetland, the most northerly part of the British Isles, crofters have traditionally managed both their moorlands and their arable land in ways which have helped support nationally important populations of many wading birds - including Britain's only regularly breeding pair of black-tailed godwit of the Icelandic race, some 80-90 per cent of Britain's small population of red-necked phalarope and 95 per cent of Britain's whimbrel. Agricultural policy changes of the type advocated in this paper would help sustain Shetland's moorland, heathland and wetland habitats, and go some way to reversing the loss of habitat due to agricultural intensification which has occurred in recent decades. Shetland's seas are much richer and more productive than its land, supporting important populations of seabirds such as great and arctic skua and arctic tern. An environmentally sensitive agricultural policy should ideally be accompanied by an environmentally sensitive policy for the management of fisheries and aquaculture, seabird populations being extremely vulnerable to overfishing.

C H Gomersall/RSPB

All of Britain's whimbrel nest in the crofting counties

1.22

From this perspective, those features which were once thought to constitute the crofting system's weaknesses are revealed as strengths. Thus the small size of crofts is a nonsense in production terms. But by enabling crofting areas to retain comparatively high numbers of people and by allowing these people to combine their farming with other occupations, the proliferation of part-time holdings in localities like the Hebrides, the West Highland mainland and Shetland has made it possible for these places to have highly diversified rural communities of the type now desired widely elsewhere.

1.23

There is a similar connection between the small-scale, low-input nature of crofting agriculture and the extent to which crofting communities exist alongside, and in conjunction with, some of Europe's most outstanding natural habitats. Thus traditional management techniques practiced over very many crofting generations have, for example, preserved the flower-rich, bird-rich machairs of the Hebrides. Indeed management of this type is essential to maintain this internationally unique resource - abandonment or intensification would quickly result in the loss of this environmental interest.

1.24

The environmental attractiveness of the crofting areas is closely bound up with the type of agriculture practiced by crofters. Crofting communities, by and large, did not engage in agricultural intensification of the type which has so radically altered the character of much of the rest of the British countryside in the course of the twentieth century. That is why the Highlands and Islands as a whole are now so important from an ornithological point of view. And that is why the corncrake, which was comparatively common throughout Britain some 70 or 80 years ago, is now largely confined to the Hebrides (see figure 1.2).

Cut and stacked hay, Kilpheder, S Uist

The Distinctive Machair of the Hebrides

Machair is the single most distinctive contribution which the crofting areas make to the natural environment. Here and there in Lewis, more generally in Harris and more universally still in islands like the Uists, Barra, Vatersay, Tiree and Iona, the sea and wind together have carried far inland great quantities of glittering white sand. When you run it through your fingers, it can be seen to consist of the crushed and pulverised remnants of innumerable shells. This sand is rich in calcium carbonate. It neutralises and fertilises the highly acidic peat with which it comes in contact. All manner of herbs and flowers flourish everywhere on the resulting soils. The overall effect, rendered still more striking by the generally unproductive nature of the surrounding landscape, is approximately equivalent to that more normally associated with an oasis in the desert. In summer the machair is a place of birdsong - of corncrake, oystercatcher, ringed plover, lapwing, dunlin, snipe, redshank, skylark and corn bunting. In winter it provides for migrant waders and geese. And all year round it is managed by crofters whose traditional cropping and grazing regimes have resulted in the machair having become a much more attractive habitat to birds than would have been the case if these grasslands had been left simply to their own devices.

Figure 1.2:   Retreat of the corncrake.

The shading indicates the regular and widespread occurence of the corncrake in
(a) 1938-9, (b) 1968-72, (c) 1978-9 and (d) 1991.

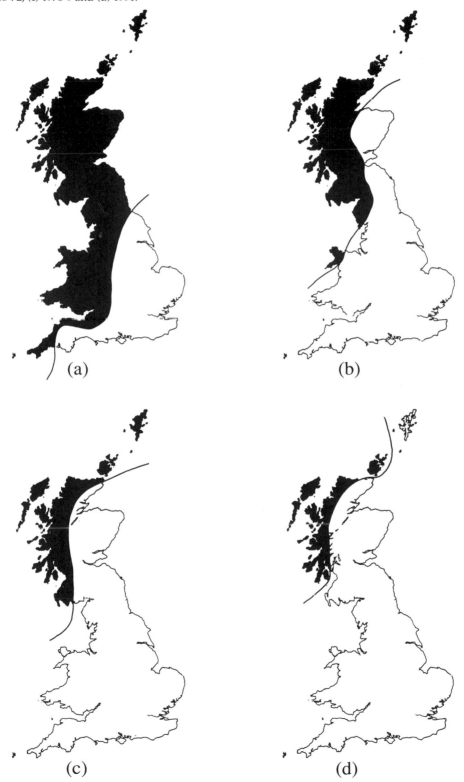

Something of the way in which crofting communities have traditionally valued
landscape, place and nature can be detected in this extract from a Gaelic poem
by Somhairle MacGill-eain, (Sorley MacLean).

The Island

O great island, Island of my love,
many a night of them I fancied
the great ocean itself restless
agitated with love of you
as you lay on the sea,
great beautiful bird of Scotland,
your supremely beautiful wings bent
about many-nooked Loch Bracadale,
your beautiful wings prostrate on the sea
from the Wild Stallion to the Aird of Sleat,
your joyous wings spread
about Loch Snizort and the world.

O great Island, my Island, my love
many a night I lay stretched
by your side in that slumber
when the mist of twilight swathed you.
My love every leaflet of heather on you
from Rudha Hunish to Loch Slapin,
and every leaflet of bog-myrtle
from Stron Bhiornaill to the Garsven,
every tarn, stream and burn a joy
from Romisdale to Brae Eynort,
and even if I came in sight of Paradise,
what price its moon without Blaven?

An t-Eilean

O Eilein mhòir, Eilean mo ghaoil,
is iomadh oidhche dhiubh a shaoil
liom an cuan mòr fhèin bhith luasgan
le do ghaol-sa air a bhuaireadh
is tu 'nad laighe air an fhairge,
eòin mhòir sgiamhaich na h-Albann,
do sgiathan àlainn air an lùbadh
mu Loch Bhràcadail ioma-chùilteach,
do sgiathan bòidheach ri muir sleuchdte
bho 'n Eist Fhiadhaich gu Aird Shlèite,
do sgiathan aoibhneach air an sgaoileadh
mu Loch Shnigheasort 's mu 'n t-saoghal!

O Eilein mhòir, m' eilein, mo chiall,
's iomadh oidhche shìn mi riamh
ri do thaobh-sa anns an t-suain ud
is ceò na camhanaich 'gad shuaineadh!
Is gràdhach liom gach bileag fraoich ort
bho Rudha Hùnais gu Loch Shlaopain,
agus gach bileag roid dhomh càirdeach
o shròin Bhiornaill gus a' Ghàrsbheinn,
gach lochan, sruth is abhainn aoibhneach
o Ròmasdal gu Bràigh Aoineart,
agus ged a nochdainn Pàrras
dè b' fhiach a ghealach-san gun Bhlàbheinn?

CHAPTER TWO

CROFTING *IN 2010*

2.1

This Chapter looks forward to the year 2010 and presents a vision of how crofting areas could appear, from the perspective of a writer in 2010. We cannot describe solutions to every problem; much discussion, consultation, negotiation and persuasion are still required to complete these details. However, the crofting community and environment described here are, we believe, attainable - the first steps to achieving them are suggested in Chapter Three.

2.2

By 2010, there have been changes in national political priorities, which have led to a general presumption that public resources are channelled only to environmentally acceptable projects, and to a recognition of the environmental value of crofting. Consequently there has been greater investment by the UK government and the European Community in developing the rural infrastructure, particularly transport, information technology and the processing and marketing of farm produce.

2.3

There have been radical but necessary changes to the financial support mechanisms for agriculture, including reform of the Common Agricultural Policy in the 1990s. The emphasis of agricultural support has switched away from production, favouring instead environmentally sensitive farming of the kind often typified by crofting.

2.4

Geography and climate in the crofting areas still strongly influence agricultural activities, and although electronic communications have improved, distance to large markets still adds an extra cost to all goods. Thus, agricultural activities in crofting areas remain heavily dependent on financial support, in common with other parts of the periphery of Europe. However, this support is justified on environmental grounds, not solely on the basis of food production.

2.5

Crofters remain in occupation of those lands which were under crofting tenure towards the close of the twentieth century. But crofting, or something very like it, has expanded into other parts of the Highlands and Islands - while changes in rural and agricultural policy have also resulted in part-time farming and smallholding becoming more common elsewhere in the United Kingdom. In both the old and new crofting areas, land is now managed in a more environmentally sensitive way. Reforms in crofting administration have resulted both in crofting communities having greater control of their own affairs, and in a much higher proportion of croft land being in active occupancy.

2.6

Crofter housing standards have improved and the introduction of more imaginative rural housing strategies has resulted in younger people finding it easier to obtain homes in their own localities. In the crofting areas, as elsewhere, houses are more energy-efficient and are designed and built in ways which both utilise much higher proportions of local materials and take account of indigenous architectural styles and traditions.

The crofter housing scheme has allowed many crofters to build and own a family home

2.7

The trend reversing long term emigration, visible in the 1980s in some areas, is accelerating and spreading. The population is increasing as young people return from periods of education and experience elsewhere to take up crofts. More young people are involved in crofting now than in the 1980s. The financial incentives for environmentally sensitive farming make crofting more worthwhile, though the majority of most crofters' income is still derived from off-croft activities. Off-croft employment opportunities have improved and, as the population grows, the service requirements increase, bringing more jobs and greater prosperity.

2.8

'Traditional' employment includes fishing, sustainable marine fish farming, weaving and knitting, and harvesting of seaweed. There is more local involvement in the management of the fishery resources, which are now managed to the benefit of the local community and the conservation of fish stocks. Fish farming has seen advances in the control of disease and parasites, but with more stringent controls on pollution and the use of chemicals. The market for farmed fish and for shellfish is stronger now with the growing consumer trend to eat more fish and less red meat. Weaving and knitwear industries continue on a small scale mainly in Lewis and Harris and in Shetland.

The Gaelic language thrives in some crofting communities

Renewable energy sources can be environmentally acceptable and provide local employment

2.9

Service employment includes transport industries, education and training, shops and suppliers, hotel and other tourist accommodation, tourist services such as pottery and crafts, and local authority services and administration. Investment in improved air, ferry and road links has increased the ease of travel to the more distant areas, bringing economic benefits, as well as more visitors. Increased leisure time, coupled with good marketing of the scenery and wildlife, is also encouraging tourism.

2.10

'New' areas of employment, of the kind first evident in the 1980s, are expanding substantially. These include home computing, publishing, promotion of Gaelic, nature conservation and mineral quarrying. Incentives to promote renewable energy generation have made windpower economic, and there are many wind generators, with a consequent need for support services. Cheap, powerful personal computers allow computer-based working from home in a wide range of subjects. Good electronic communications networks provide opportunities for a range of businesses, training and learning. The Gaelic language and culture is a growth area in some parts of the crofting counties. Some young crofters, with the required skills and training, are employed directly in nature conservation work. There are also seasonal employment opportunities to show the wildlife and the landscape to visitors.

Off-croft employment is essential in maintaining crofting's viability

2.11

Crofting is still a part-time activity. Where employment is home-based, time off for crofting activities is not a problem. For off-croft employment, there are novel schemes to allow crofters to have a job and to have sufficient time for croft work. These include a greater willingness by employers to allow unpaid leave for crofting activities without jeopardising the employment, and a higher proportion of crofters working on a range of other jobs on a self-employed basis. Much of the free time for crofting is achieved by extending to the crofting areas the kinds of job sharing schemes already common elsewhere in the 1980s. During the main periods of croft activity - silage or hay time, for example - the township organises sharing of the cutting to allow efficient use of machines and the least disruption for those unable to leave their other work.

2.12

Crofting is more securely based than ever before. Undoubtedly rural development funds have played their part, but the main cause is the change in agricultural support. These have revitalised crofting, lifting it from its dependence on the poor sheep market of the early 1990s to the more diversified farming economy of the twenty first century. The fundamental

Traditional industries such as weaving complement crofting's part-time nature

Shetland is famous for its knitwear

Tourism provides a growing market for the craft industry

Crofting is essentially a community activity

change has been the recognition by national and European government that environmentally sensitive farming is worth greater support than farming for maximum output. The support mechanisms are principally agricultural, although Scottish Natural Heritage and the Forest Authority also provide grants. Other financial support and advice is provided by the Highlands and Islands Enterprise and local government. All support is now provided through a coordinated and simplified administrative structure.

2.13

Farmers are free to chose from a range of support options. In crofting areas, the option carrying the highest support is environmentally sensitive farming. This reflects the high conservation value of these areas, and many crofters have taken advantage of the support to diversify and improve the quality of their crofting activities.

2.14

The vegetation cover in croftig areas now reflects a particular management strategy chosen by each crofter, or by the township. Derelict and under-used land is uncommon, and there are fewer absentees; changes in the legislation have resulted in improved use of crofting land.

2.15

Part of today's livestock support is linked to the ratio of sheep to cattle, and favours cattle more than in the 1980s. Where suitable, in-bye areas are grazed by the increased numbers of beef and dairy cattle that have become the mainstay of the economy of several townships. These animals provide beef for market, and milk is sold locally. Many areas are grazed throughout the year. Grants are available for the construction or repair of outbuildings to provide milking sheds, shelter and in-wintering.

Livestock and Wildlife

Environmental interests are best served by an appropriate mix of cattle and sheep grazing at a stocking rate that is sustainable in the long term. Cattle tend to leave a taller sward, which adds to diversity, and in damp ground poaching benefits waders like lapwing, redshank and snipe which nest in these areas. Around the fields, drainage ditches with iris beds provide cover for waders, corncrakes and other wildlife, especially early in the breeding season.

2.16

Most townships now grow grass as winter feed for livestock, often on in-bye but also on the machair (see 2.22). The incentive comes from the silage/hay premium scheme, which was devised in the 1990s. This scheme supports silage and hay production, provided it is cut late. It has tiered payments which reflect the date of harvesting: the later the date the higher the payment, in recognition of the decline with age in digestibility. The scheme also provides payments for the way in which a field is harvested and for leaving small margins uncut around the edges of fields. Harvesting is done usually in strips, and never by cutting from the outside of the field spiralling inwards. This scheme has helped save the corncrake which is now spreading back to the mainland.

Low intensity agricultural management sustains a rich environment

John Charity

Hay-cutting on the machair : such traditional management deserves support

Red-necked Phalarope

Fewer than 20 pairs of red-necked phalarope now breed in Britain, all in crofting areas. They breed in small marshes or lochans with a mix of open water and abundant emergent vegetation. The maintenance of an appropriate water level and a mosaic of vegetation, by low intensity grazing at the right time of year, is essential for the conservation of this species.

2.21

In the wetter areas, many crofts include small lochans or marshes. The marshes are often of considerable conservation importance and are left undisturbed. Streams are unpolluted by slurry or other waste and care is taken to balance the need for drainage with the conservation interest.

2.22

The machair (see definition in Chapter One) is an area of great nature conservation interest, and is confined mainly to the Hebridean islands. Traditionally it was an area cultivated for crops such as hay, cereals and potatoes, as a mixture of common land and strip workings in summer, and grazed in the winter. In the 1980s, much of the machair was fenced and apportioned. Some of these fences are no longer maintained and have been removed, as the need for them has disappeared through better control of grazing by the township. Late-cut silage is now more popular than hay, but cereals and some root crops are still grown, and in winter the machair is still lightly grazed.

2.23

The total extent of silage and hay is much greater now than in the 1990s, thanks to the premium scheme. In some townships about half the farmed machair is given over to these meadows, where the corncrake thrives. The premium is available even on small areas. Some meadows are rye grass, while others have a range of native grasses and other wild flowers. Even the rye grass leys revert to a semi-natural state after a few years, so reseeding needs to be done periodically. This is done under the premium scheme, with the scale

John Charity

Crofters will play an important part in the future of the machair

C H Gomersall/RSPB

Red-necked phalarope

Murdo McLeod

More cattle would benefit the machair

moorland is increasingly seen as an asset. Birds of prey and skuas are allowed to breed undisturbed. Some nests, which can be viewed without disturbance, are used to show to visitors. The golden eagle in particular attracts much interest. Such initiatives are run by crofters in conjunction with conservation organisations, and provide additional income.

2.31

In the 1990s much of the produce of the croft was sold for finishing outside the crofting areas. Then, the identity of the produce grown in an environmentally sensitive way was lost among produce from the worst examples of farming. In the townships today some processing facilities for livestock exist, to allow the marketing of produce distinctly associated with crofting. These facilities are shared by several townships and are supported by the demand outwith the crofting counties for produce with an environmentally sensitive label. However, the consumer is still mainly driven by cost, and the competition for markets is intense, so much effort continues to be invested in marketing

2.32

One reason for the continued support of crofting is the great conservation interest of crofting areas. Crofters are the custodians of some of the best wildlife areas of the UK and are thus the producers of 'goods' which society values. These 'goods' include habitats that are rich in wildlife, an attractive and unpolluted landscape,

a rich culture, access for recreation and food. And, many of these 'goods' are directly affected by agricultural support.

2.33

Another benefit of this continued support is the help it provides for the economically disadvantaged areas in the Highlands and Islands. This aid has prevented the collapse of agriculture and ensured that the crofting areas have continued to be managed. Without support, further emigration to urban areas and/or social payments are the only options. Also, the cultural diversity in crofting areas is widely recognised.

2.34

The means of support are very different from the 1980s. The reform of the CAP has made financial support available for environmentally sensitive farming. Thus crofters, in common with environmentally sensitive farmers throughout Europe, are supported by a series of grants and incentives, and crofting areas receive the highest payments available because they produce an environment of the highest conservation value.

CHAPTER THREE

SUPPORTING CROFTING

3.1

This Chapter assesses the public support currently made available to crofting areas and argues that reform would significantly contribute to achieving the vision of crofting outlined in Chapter Two. We also argue that, given the increasing emphasis on conservation in both European and UK land use policy, the crofting areas which are so valuable for conservation are worthy of modest increases in public support.

CURRENT SUPPORT FOR LAND USE IN CROFTING AREAS

3.2

The crofting areas are designated as Less Favoured Areas (LFAs) in terms of agricultural production; that is

areas "in danger of depopulation and where the conservation of the countryside is necessary" (Article 4, COM 75/268). The crofting counties are also considered an objective 5b area in terms of the EC's rural development policy (under COM 2052/88); that is a region with particular problems in agriculture.

3.3

Crofters are, therefore, eligible for a range of support measures aimed at land use, including the basic support for livestock production available to all farmers. There are also two schemes specifically targeted at crofting (the Crofting Counties Agricultural Grants (Scotland) Scheme and the Crofters Building Grants and Loans Scheme).

3.4

Allegedly, crofting receives large quantities of public support from the EC and the UK government. We believe this claim is exaggerated and argue that the increasing emphasis on maintaining populations in rural areas, and on protecting and enhancing the environment means that crofting is receiving less than its fair share of public expenditure.

3.5

Figure 3.1 gives an estimate of the total public expenditure associated with crofting land use over the last nine years (the period for which all figures could be obtained) and shows the relative importance of the various types of support. The main elements of support over the last decade have

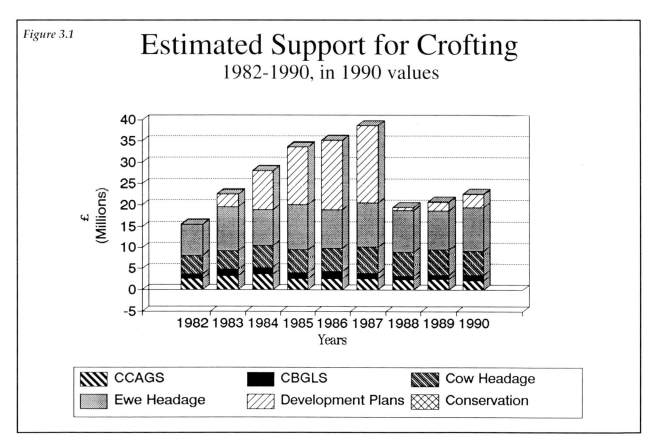

Figure 3.1

Estimated Support for Crofting
1982-1990, in 1990 values

£ (Millions)

Years

CCAGS   CBGLS   Cow Headage
Ewe Headage   Development Plans   Conservation

been headage payments under the Common Agricultural Policy and special, regionally targeted development programmes. In 1990, we estimated that support totalled £23.5 million; equivalent to only one tenth of the expenditure on oilseed support in the United Kingdom (MAFF, 1992), although the area of oilseed rape is half that of the crofting areas.

3.6

The Crofting Counties Agricultural Grants (Scotland) Scheme estimate has ranged between £1.7 and £2.7 million. In 1990, almost a third of this money was spent on land improvement and another third on farm equipment. A further quarter was spent on fencing and the remainder on drainage and amenities. The estimate for Crofters Building Grants and Loans Scheme only includes the grants component (ie excludes loans) and has varied from £0.8 to £1.5 million.

3.7

Sheep headage payments include Hill Sheep Compensatory Allowances and Sheep Annual Premium payments, amounting to £4.5 and £6.0 million respectively in 1990. The cow headage payments include Hill Cow Compensatory Allowances and the Suckler Cow Premium, accounting for £3.2 and £2.5 million respectively. Not surprisingly, given the dominance of sheep in the crofting areas, sheep headage payments total almost twice those for cattle.

3.8

The Development Programmes include the Western Isles Integrated Development Programme (IDP), the Scottish Islands Agricultural Development Programme (ADP), the Skye Development Programme and the North West Development Programme. Estimates for the IDP include grants for farm and livestock

development, but exclude those for fish farming, crofter housing and infrastructure, as we are largely considering land use here. The money attached to each scheme tends to build up towards its completion, as more plans come to fruition. The IDP cost £6.6 million in 1984, rising to £14.6 million in 1987; the ADP cost only £0.6 million in 1988, but £2.9 million in 1990.

3.9

The conservation section (which hardly shows up on the chart) includes payments under management agreements for Environmentally Sensitive Areas (ESAs) and Sites of Special Scientific Interest (SSSIs). The ADP also includes a conservation element, in the form of environmental management payments, amounting to 13% of the total payments under this programme or around £0.4

A PART-TIME CROFTER with a full-time professional job in the Western Isles. Works 3 crofts, with 8 ha inbye, 6 ha apportioned. Keeps 60 breeding ewes; grows 1 ha of oats, rye, barley and potatoes; buys in hay.

About one-fifth of his income comes from the croft, much the same as 10 years ago. Of this grants and subsidies account for about 35%. He would like transport subsidies to be introduced "especially for people like ourselves who are far from the markets. Buyers coming here are affected too. Buying feed is really expensive: a tonne of hay costs ú100, double the cost on the mainland."

One of the current problems in crofting, he thinks, is people keeping on their sheep for too long in order to receive the sheep subsidies. Another problem is that the rules and regulations all seem to come from Edinburgh. He would prefer it to be more localised.

He can see both pros and cons to the 1976 Crofting Reform (Scotland) Act. People buying their crofts and selling them for house sites is a good source of income for the crofter, as long as he is indifferent to his neighbours. One of the benefits of the Act is that a crofter can give a site to one of his children to build a house.

million for crofters. The fact that altogether conservation grants account for a maximum of only £0.7 million, or 3% of the total support paid in 1990, indicates the lack of importance attached to conservation by the funding agencies. We believe conservation payments are a great untapped area of potential revenue for crofting areas and look forward to this area of expenditure increasing.

COMPARISON OF A CROFT AND A FARM

3.10

In order to put this level and type of support in context, we can compare it with support to agriculture elsewhere. Table 3a compares an average croft (from A Survey of Crofting Incomes, Kinloch and Dalton, 1990) with an average full-time LFA livestock farm in Scotland (from the Farm Account Survey, MAFF 1991a). The croft is about one-fifth of the size of the farm in terms of area, but has less than one-tenth of the output and provides only one-twentieth of the income. (Even when converted to a per 100 ewe equivalent basis, where one rearing cow is assumed to be equal to 7.5 ewes, the net farm income is nearly 3 times as much on farms as on crofts.) Although direct grants and subsidies account for a larger proportion of income and output than on the farm, the actual figure, under £900, is only 13% of the £7000 of direct support received by the farm.

3.11

Crofts are at a disadvantage to these larger farms with whom they must compete when selling their marketable produce. Location is probably the greatest constraint on crofting, partly because the weather is so unfavourable to agricultural production (for example, Skye has 240 cm of rainfall per year), and partly because of the distance from markets, entailing expensive freight charges, especially to and from the islands. For instance, it currently costs £21.50 to ship a cow from Stornoway on Lewis to Ullapool on the mainland, and £1.50 for each lamb. From Lerwick on Shetland to Aberdeen the freight costs are even more prohibitive at £33 a cow and £5 a lamb. Similarly, transport costs are high for importing hay and other foodstuffs. These factors contribute to a relatively low enterprise output: £29 per ewe compared with £37-41 per ewe for Scotland as a whole (Kinloch and Dalton, 1990).

3.12

Crofts, as smaller units, are at a disadvantage, with both lower outputs and higher costs. The latter is for several reasons: crofters are not able to make use of discounts available for bulk purchases; often they cannot buy inputs in suitably small quantities; and small-scale equipment is not available, so that fixed costs, such as machinery expenses, are higher.

3.13

One of the effects of being in a remote area is that crofters have traditionally had to be self-reliant. Although only a small area of land is cropped, because of the shortage of suitable land and the harsh climate, the cereals that are grown (most frequently a black oat/rye mix) are used for livestock feed. Grass conservation is also important, in order to reduce the necessity to buy in feed for the winter months. A limiting factor on cattle stocks is often the quantity of locally-conserved winter fodder. Potatoes are mostly grown in small areas for household consumption, and nearly half the crofts in the income survey slaughtered some of their stock for home consumption.

High transport costs are a severe disadvantage for crofters

Table 3a
Comparison of a Croft and a full-time livestock farm in the Scottish Less Favoured Area
(Average per holding per annum) (1)

	CROFT 1989	LFA LIVESTOCK FARM 1989/90
Areas:		
Total area (ha)	89	395
of which % rough grazing	84	82
Average adjusted area (ha)	22	103
Number of beef cows	4	47
Number of ewes	91	349
Total livestock units	17	112
Stocking Density	0.77	1.09
Hours on the holding	939	2638
Hours off the holding	1366	218
Output (£):		
Crops	167	6300
Livestock	4153	43700
Misc	376	3100
Total Output	4697	53100
Total Inputs (£)	4137	43400
Net Farm Income (£)	560	9700
Occupier Income (£):		
Crofting	326	7500
Non-crofting		
— earned on the croft	241	900
— earned outside the croft	6218	1100
— unearned (eg pensions)	1866	1400
Total non-croft	8325	3400
Total occupier income	8650	10900
Direct Grants and Subsidies (£) (2)	869	7000
— as % of net farm income	155.2	72.2
— as % of total output	18.5	13.2
— as % of livestock output	20.9	16.0
Returns to labour (£/hr):		
From holding	0.35	2.84
From off-holding	4.73	9.17
(excludes unearned income)		

(1) Figures are averages for 65 crofts and 255 LFA livestock farms, except for occupier income figures, which refer to 65 crofts and 137 farms.

(2) Grants and subsidies for specific enterprises, largely headage payments

Source: Kinloch and Dalton (1990)

3.14

Most crofts only need to be worked part-time, with many crofters using the croft to supplement their income from other sources, whether that be other work or a retirement pension. On average, crofters spend 40% of their time working on the croft (Kinloch and Dalton, 1990). Throughout Europe this is not unusual; in 1985, 30% of farmers in the Community of Ten supplemented their farming income with other activities, either on their own premises or by off-farm employment on a part-time or full-time basis (Commission of the European Community, 1988). The importance of part-time units should not be underestimated; crofts account for over 20% of agricultural output from the seven crofting counties and over 25% of the total agricultural land area (The Crofters Commission, 1991).

3.15

The return for the hours spent working on the croft is very low, only 35 pence per hour, compared to an hourly rate of almost £5 earned off the croft. LFA livestock farms, however, earn £2.84 per hour on the farm and as much as £9.17 off the farm. This indicates that crofters are not crofting for solely financial reasons and that they have less well-paid employment opportunities off the holding. However, the level of support, and hence income, are factors in whether the crofter is able to continue crofting.

THE INFLUENCE OF SUPPORT ON CROFTING

3.16

We argue that crofting is directed by the amount and type of public support even though this is not always beneficial to crofting. This is not a new phenomenon. In 1947, Frank Fraser Darling, while discussing the increase in sheep-stocking in the Hebrides, noted that, "The economic situation is wholly artificial, brought about by the ewe subsidy... but the conditions of overgrazing are real and dangerous" (Darling FF, 1955).

3.17

The following analysis uses Agricultural Census data for crofts and small farms (up to 16 British Size Units), which can be counted as holdings of like economic status. This will not cover all crofts, as the Census does not cover insignificant holdings

(those below 1 hectare and 1 BSU). However, the latest figures available for insignificant holdings (covering probably 80% of them) show that they account for only 13% of the total area, 24% of the breeding ewes and 8% of beef cows on all crofts and small farms. Census data should therefore give a good indication of the general trends in crofting land use.

3.18

Most of the crofting land is rough grazing - 88.5% in 1990. Figure 3.2 shows the other land uses over the period 1982 to 1990. Permanent grazing accounts for 62,000 hectares, or 39% of the area excluding rough grazing. Temporary grazing (less than 5 years old) has remained fairly constant at around 15,000 hectares. The area cut for hay and silage has fluctuated around 28,000 hectares. There has been an increase in the area of woodland to 20,000 hectares and the total area of crops has fallen to 11,000 hectares.

3.19

A closer look at the changes in crops (figure 3.3) shows that the area of oats, crops for stockfeeding and barley have all fallen considerably since 1982 (by 39%, 21% and 11% respectively). This fall in cropping coincides with the discontinuance of the Marginal Cropping Grant. Currently, support for cereals is solely through the CAP, with prices of wheat, barley, maize, rye and sorghum supported primarily through the use of intervention buying. The much greater move away from oats may be partly due to oat prices not being supported in this way.

3.20

The Marginal Cropping Grant was changed in 1967 to a choice between the cropping grants and the Supplementary Headage Payment for hill cattle and/or hill sheep. This emphasised livestock at the expense of cropping and the area of tillage

---

A FULL-TIME CROFTER for 9 months of the year in Ross-shire, a full-time fisherman for the other 3 months. Works 9 crofts, with 20 ha in-bye land and 40 ha apportioned land. 580 breeding ewes, no crops.

Fifteen years ago the croft used to have 8 cows, and grew turnips, potatoes, hay and corn. However, the cattle and cropping became uneconomic. Timewise, the cattle were difficult to fit in with the fishing - there was no longer a bull coming to the township and the Marginal Cropping Grant was stopped. The arable land has reverted to rough grazing - "our sheep are on the hill all summer so we don't control our in-bye by grazing it, like we did when it was cropped."

"In this era of privatisation, tenure has become a dirty word. But the importance of crofting is that it is the most unique system of land tenure in the whole world. It has served for one hundred years, and has been the only sustainable thing that we, its people, have had in the Highlands. It should be preserved and guarded on that basis."

For economic stability in crofting, he believes, a ten year commitment from government is required. "You cannot run a business by changing it from day to day."

"What keeps me crofting? An overdraft that I can't get rid of."

Figure 3.2

Land Uses in Crofting Areas
Source: June Census, 1-16 BSU Holdings

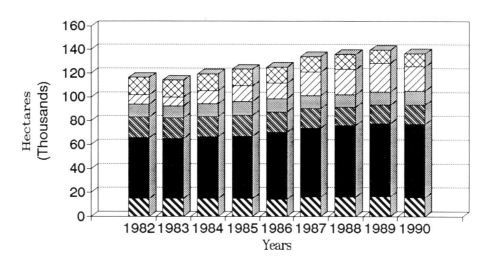

Figure 3.3

Crop Areas in Crofting Areas
Source: June Census, 1-16 BSU holdings

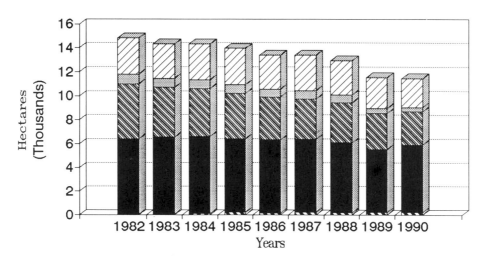

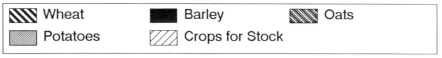

42

immediately fell by 1,329 hectares. The area of tillage fell by over 70% between 1965 and 1976 (from 11,381 hectares to only 3,279 hectares) (Crofters Commission, pers. comm.). The grant was eventually discontinued in 1981 because of the continuing decline in uptake. Given the low level of payments for tillage relative to livestock, it is not surprising that the area of tillage decreased, leading to a low uptake.

3.21

Similarly livestock numbers have been influenced by headage payments. Figure 3.4 shows the relative headage payments for beef cows and ewes over the last 20 years in 1990 values (DAFS Annual Reports). In 1970, the support for a beef cow was 18 times that for a ewe; now it is only 7 times. This ratio is likely to become even lower with the withdrawal of the variable premium on fat lambs from the beginning of 1992 and the compensatory rise in ewe premium payments. As most lambs from crofts are sold on as stores, rather than sold fat, the ewe premium has a more direct effect, whilst the variable premium has only indirectly supported crofting through its knock-on effect on store prices.

3.22

Figure 3.5 shows the change in livestock numbers in the crofting counties for all significant sizes of croft and farm (Nairn, Bute and Arran statistical areas have been excluded from the HIDB figures to make them comparable with the 1990 figures). Over the period 1970 to 1990, the number of beef cows fell by 6% and

Agricultural support has favoured sheep at the expense of a more balanced crofting economy

the number of breeding ewes increased by 14%, leading to a considerable fall in the cattle to sheep ratio. This trend appears to reflect the economic signals given to crofters by the relative headage payments. Unfortunately, as sheep are harder grazers than cattle, this has increased the pressures of overgrazing in many areas, reducing further the productiveness of the land.

3.23

These changes are also partly driven by the changes in the number of people and crofts. Between 1960 and 1985, the number of registered crofts fell by 10%, while the number of crofters fell by 23% (Revell et al, 1987). Many crofters are tenants of more than one croft, and there are a considerable number of absentee crofters (1,100 are known to the Crofters Commission). There are now around 9,000 active crofters (SCU) and 17,671 registered crofts (Crofters Commission, 1990).

Figure 3.4

Ewe versus Cow Headage Payments
(Maximum HIDB rates at 1990 prices)

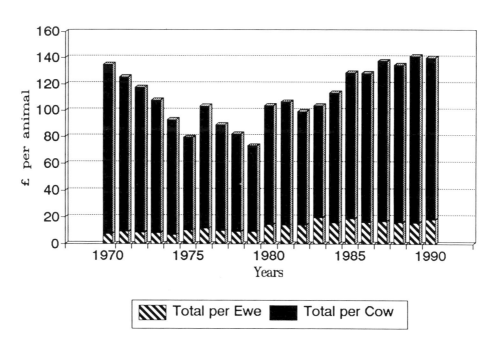

Figure 3.5

No of livestock in the Crofting Areas
Source: Revell et al, 1987; CC, 1991

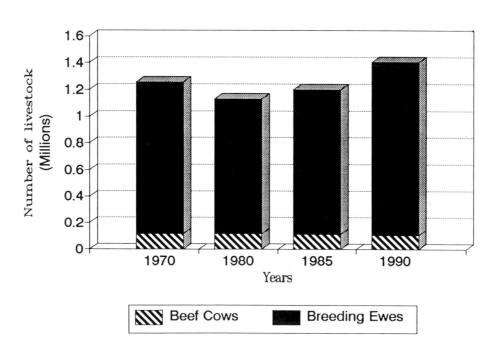

3.24

One of the major changes since the 1976 Crofting Reform (Scotland) Act has been the increase in owner occupation to a level of at least 15%. (This is probably an underestimate as not all changes to owner occupation are notified to the Crofters Commission.) The level of owner occupation varies considerably between areas, generally increasing towards the east and ranging from hardly any in the Western Isles to 65% in Orkney (Crofters Commission, 1990).

3.25

One of the most significant effects of the increase in owner occupation has been to allow more land to be transferred from one owner to another without its associated house, as bareland croft. The Crofters Commission has no control over the succession of owner-occupied crofts. Of recent assignations, less than one-third of assignees now live on or intend building a house and living on the assigned croft. It is estimated that 500 crofts lose their associated house in any one year (Arkleton Trust, 1990).

New Objectives For Crofting Support

3.26

Chapter One showed the importance of crofting in nurturing a rich, diverse wildlife, a beautiful landscape, and in sustaining a population and its cultures in remote and harsh areas of Britain, together with the maintenance of the Gaelic language in the west. All these attributes can be termed 'public goods', as any individual's consumption of such a good does not detract from another's consumption of that good. For example, one person's enjoyment of the sound of a corncrake calling neither excludes nor prevents another person enjoying the same call. Conventional markets for goods and services cannot deal with this type of 'public good', partly because as long as people cannot be excluded from consuming a good, they will not be willing to pay for its consumption. As markets generally use prices to decide the level of provision they will tend to provide not enough or, worse still, no public goods at all. As the market will not provide public goods satisfactorily, the government must intervene and provide public support for the provision of these goods and services.

3.27

In the last few years there has been increasing recognition from both the UK government and the EC that the reasons for supporting rural areas must be broadened beyond food production, and maintenance of farmers' incomes, to include the provision of public goods and services for the benefit of society as a whole. UK Agriculture Departments recently stated in *Our Farming Future* that 'The objectives of the CAP should be adjusted to give greater recognition to the importance of environmental protection. The CAP should develop so that it can be as successful in benefiting the environment as it has been in encouraging the production of food. To this end support should be directed towards more environmentally sensitive farming practices. ..... The Government intends to link financial support more closely to environmental benefits.' (MAFF, 1991c).

AN ABSENTEE CROFTER, with a full time professional job in Aberdeen and a croft in Lewis.

She inherited the croft 10 years ago. Although brought up on a croft, someone from outside the family always had the use of it (unofficially). She left Lewis to go to university in Aberdeen, found a job and married there. She cannot see herself and her husband moving back to Lewis. "There are no jobs for our careers in the island."

A local crofter has the use of her croft for grazing sheep. "We have a partnership between us: I don't charge him rent, but in the past we have shared the cost of fencing and reseeding." She has considered subletting the croft legally, but likes to retain control over it. "Being an islander is a part of me" and "I'd like to keep the croft in case our own children might want to use it."

3.28

Similarly, in 1988 in *The Future of Rural Society*, the EC Commission said 'In the context of rural development, the constructive role which agriculture and forestry can play in the protection of the rural environment must be emphasised. In so far as these activities are thus sources of a necessary and valuable 'public good', there is a case for environmental incentives or compensation, which might in certain circumstances have a permanent character' (Commission of the EC, 1988).

3.29

More recently, in its proposals to reform the CAP, the Commission recognised 'that there would be advantage in doing this in a manner which would reduce production and reflect greater concern for the environment, that there should be a better distribution of support among farmers taking into account the difficulties of some categories of producers and regions, that more specific incentives towards environmentally friendly farming should be available, that there should be greater recognition of the dual role of the farmer in producing food and managing the countryside, that non-food use of agricultural products should be encouraged and that better incentives should be available for farmers to take early retirement'.

3.30

Is this just rhetoric? There is already a considerable amount of public financial support made to crofting, as outlined in figure 3.1. However the majority of this is still aimed at food production, through headage payments, despite the good intentions of agriculture departments and the EC. Very little support, perhaps 3%, is directly aimed at the provision of public goods. Given the changing objectives behind public support for rural areas, the direction and form of that support also needs to be changed. As support is increasingly directed towards conservation rather than production, areas such as the crofting counties, which tend to be marginal in terms of production but central in terms of conservation, should gain a greater proportion of public support.

3.31

The Royal Society for the Protection of Birds (Taylor and Dixon, 1990) have proposed that public support can be redirected to meet the new objectives of government intervention in rural areas, through the mechanism of cross compliance. Cross compliance means making

---

DIVERSIFIED CROFTER who combines crofting with creel fishing in Sutherland. Works 3 crofts with 28 ha of in-bye and outrun land. Keeps 3 horses, 15 sheep, 3 goats and 40 hens and grows 2 ha of hay, turnips and organic vegetables.

Sells goat's milk, yogurt and soft cheeses, eggs and organic vegetables. Tries to have the hay cut by midsummer's night, and in the barn by the end of June. "I used to cut it later on in the year, but the weather is pretty bad and I get better hay with an early cut." Uses seaweed on the main small cropping area, and shell sand as a lime on the peaty areas. He likes having a variety of stock, and is planning to move into cattle. One of the main problems today, he believes, is the monoculture of sheep, causing overgrazing and making it difficult to manipulate the grazing pattern.

"Crofting has deteriorated over the last two decades by relying wholly on sheep - that's a personal view. There's less of a commitment from the crofter to sheep than there is to cattle or crops. From a purely economic point of view, crofters made the right decision by going into sheep. But with the collapse in the market, this has left crofting very vulnerable. Instead of being subsidised to produce sheep, we could be equally subsidised to go into, for example, rotation or crop production."

He considers that the 1976 Crofting Reform (Scotland) Act has weakened the crofting base. Crofters have failed to adapt to the changes that are taking place, failed to take advantage of economic opportunities. "We have got to look at letting new entrants into crofting - many areas are failing to do this. More and more land is held by fewer crofters, and there is a lot of land lying derelict and underused."

support for a farmer's food production depend on his or her participation in one of the existing schemes to give environmental benefits. We would envisage there being three main complementary schemes:

Sensitive Farming Options: built on the system of ESAs, to sustain traditional farming systems of high conservation value, by rewarding farmers for maintaining these, and helping forestall environmentally damaging intensification.

Extensive Farming Options: Reductions in grazing densities, or fertiliser use, or conversion to organic farming would modify intensive systems to reduce production and enhance the environment.

Land Diversion Options: built on the set-aside and farm woodland schemes to modify intensive farming systems, reduce production and divert land to new uses including habitat re-creation.

3.32

Each crofter, along with all other farmers, would be free to choose to join one of these schemes and, in return, would receive agricultural support through the CAP. Thus, crofters who choose to enter an ESA-type agreement (the most likely option for crofters) would be eligible for CAP support. Such a reform would ensure that the CAP not only continues to maintain farm incomes and sustain rural communities, but also provides environmental benefits, appropriate to the local situation.

A NEW SUPPORT SCHEME FOR CROFTING

3.33

The following section looks at how a new system of support could be made to work in crofting areas, and the likely cost of changing support mechanisms in this way. The new objectives require new means of support which should be integrated, less production-oriented and more conservation-oriented. An appropriate mechanism for achieving this would be cross compliance.

● **Recommendation 1**
A new support system for crofting should be introduced, using cross compliance as the mechanism for linking all the schemes available to crofters to the provision of environmental benefits.

3.34

We suggest these changes could be made under the auspices of the accompanying measures to the reform of the CAP, proposed by the European Commission and now being discussed by the Council of Ministers (COM 91/415), which if agreed could replace the current ESA schemes (Council Regulation 2328/91). The proposed legislation could provide the basis for a Community-wide scheme, with priority given to particular regional zones. We believe that the crofting areas should be designated as a high priority region, and that the following suggestions for reforming support in the area should be introduced. This would help the implementation of the Directive on the Conservation of Wild Birds and fulfil the EC's aims of supporting objective 5b areas.

● **Recommendation 2**
Within the regional zones, proposed by the EC to accompany CAP reform, the UK government should insist that there is some degree of prioritisation, with the crofting region given highest priority.

INTEGRATION OF SUPPORT

3.35

Over the last 20 years we have identified a staggering 42 different schemes associated with land use that were available to crofters (see table 3b). Currently there are 22 different schemes in operation, involving four different government departments, Highlands and Islands Enterprise (and their network of LECs), the local authorities and the Scottish Agricultural Colleges.

The Highlands and Islands are the European stronghold of the otter

GRANT SCHEMES AVAILABLE TO CROFTERS SINCE 1970

(This may not be a comprehensive list, as information on discontinued schemes was often difficult to unearth.)

NAME	DURATION	ADMINISTRATORS
Production Grants		
Marginal Cropping Grant	1956-1981	CC (crofts) SOAFD (non-crofts)
Special Grants to Scottish Islands	1955-1984	SOAFD
Beef Cow, Hill Cattle, Upland and Hill Sheep Subsidies	1949-1976	SOAFD
Hill Sheep and Hill Cow Compensatory Allowances	1976-present (higher rates for HIDB area from 1985)	SOAFD
Winter Keep Supplementary Payments for Hill Cattle	c1970-present	SOAFD
Sheep Annual Premium Scheme	1980-present	SOAFD
Sheep Variable Premium Scheme	1980-1991	SOAFD
Suckler Cow Premium	1980-present	SOAFD
Beef Premium Scheme	1980-1989	SOAFD
Beef Special Premium	1989-present	SOAFD
Capital Grants		
Crofting Counties AgriculturalGrants (Scotland) Scheme	1956-present	CC (crofts) SOAFD (non-crofts)
Crofters Building Grants and Loans Scheme	1911-present	SOAFD
HIE Grants and Loans	1965-present	HIE
Farm Structure Scheme Ingoers and Outgoers Compensation	1968-c1980	SOAFD
Ingoers Scheme (loans)	1956-present	CC
Livestock Purchase Loans	1956-present	CC (crofts) SOAFD (non-crofts)
Outer Isles Ram Lamb Scheme	1911-present	SOAFD
Shetland Ram Scheme	1950s-present	SOAFD
Highlands and IslandsVeterinary Services Scheme	c1935-present	SOAFD
Agricultural Lime Scheme	1946-1976	SOAFD
Livestock Improvement Schemes		
Bull and Ram Supply Scheme	1897-present	SOAFD
Premium Bull Scheme	c1930-1979	SOAFD
Artificial Insemination	1961-present	SOAFD
Heifer Retention Scheme	1972-1977	HIE
Heifer Production Scheme	1977-1988	HIE
Heifer Improvement for the Isles of Lewis/Harris	1981-1990	HIE
Heifer Improvement for the Isle of Skye	1983-1990	HIE
Blackface Improvement Scheme	1990-present	HIE
Cashmere Goat Scheme	1989-present	HIE
Rural Development Schemes		
Township Roads Scheme	1897-1985	SOEnD/Local Authorities
Western Isles Integrated Development Programme	1982-1987	SOAFD/HIE/WIIC
Township Development Scheme (post IDP for completion)	1989-present	HIE/CC
Skye Development Programme	1986-1992	CC/HIE
Scottish Islands Agricultural Development Programme	1988-1993	SOAFD/HIE
North West Development Programme	1989-1993	HIE/CASE/CC/SOAFD
Rural Enterprise Programme	1991-present	HIE/SOAFD
Conservation Grants		
Sites of Special Scientific Interest	1949-present	NCCS
Environmentally Sensitive Areas	1986-present	SOAFD
Misc conservation grants eg rabbit control in the Uists, and advisory services	present	NCCS
Emergency Grants		
EC Emergency Aid for Island Producers	1979	EC/SOAFD
Temporary Assistance to Livestock Producers		
- grants for freight	1980	SOAFD
Adverse Weather Aid	1986	SOAFD

KEY:

CASE	-	Caithness and Sutherland Enterprise Company
CC	-	Crofters Commission
EC	-	European Commission
HIE	-	Highlands and Islands Enterprise; formerly HIDB (Highlands and Islands Development Board)
NCCS	-	Nature Conservancy Council for Scotland; formerly NCC (Nature Conservancy Council)
SOAFD	-	Scottish Office Agriculture and Fisheries Department; formerly DAFS (Department of Agriculture andFisheries for Scotland)
SOEnD	-	Scottish Office Environment Department; formerly SDD (Scottish Development Department)

The following agencies are also involved in giving financial assistance and/or advice to crofters:
Comhairle nan Eilean (Western Isles Islands Council); Shetland Islands Council; Highland Regional Council; Strathclyde Regional Council; Local Enterprise Companies; Scottish Agricultural Colleges; The Highland Fund.

RSPB

The chough depends on low-intensity, pastoral agriculture

Cailean MacGill-eain

Tomorrow's crofting community depends on attracting today's young people

3.36

With such a number of schemes and bodies involved there is inevitably a danger of duplication of administration and, more seriously, a problem of conflicting objectives between the schemes, and hence conflicting signals to crofters. For example, under the Crofting Counties Agricultural Grants (Scotland) Scheme, grants were available in 1988 of up to 70% for the improvement of land by reclamation, regeneration, laying down of permanent pasture, reseeding and reconditioning, and for access tracks to land improvement areas, and up to 55% for the provision of fences, hedges, walls and gates. Meanwhile, under the ESA and ADP management agreements, SOAFD retains the right to prevent any such land improvements, fencing or construction of vehicular tracks going ahead.

3.37

The introduction of cross compliance into support for rural areas would allow the integration of agricultural, environmental and rural development policies (including support for the Gaelic language). This would ensure that any contradictions between the various policies and the overall objectives of support for rural areas would be ironed out and that duplication would be avoided, thus minimising administration costs. Designating one organisation as the coordinating agency or contact point for crofters, in respect of all schemes, would immediately simplify the current confusing and wasteful system.

● **Recommendation 3**
A coordinating agency should be identified, to act as the contact point for crofters in respect of all schemes.

MORE CONSERVATION ORIENTED

3.38

As discussed earlier, the introduction of cross compliance into agricultural support would greatly increase the emphasis on conservation. This would be largely achieved through the extension and improvement of the ESAs system, whereby crofters are eligible for management payments for maintaining their traditional environmentally sensitive methods. However, the integration of the ESA with other agricultural support through cross compliance would make it a much more effective mechanism than at present.

3.39

We would like to see all crofters eligible to join an ESA-type scheme. All crofters could benefit from the assured income source, independent of the vagaries of the market. One of the great advantages to the crofter of an ESA-type scheme is that it allows him or her to plan ahead, knowing that there is a predictable income source for the next 5 years. We would prefer to see agreements extended to 10 or 20 years, as this would give more security to both the crofter and the crofting environment.

3.40

In addition, the only existing ESA in the crofting counties (the Machair of the Uists and Benbecula, Barra and Vatersay) is extremely limited. Only one-third of corncrakes breeding on the Uists is thought to be within the ESA boundary (Seymour, 1991). The remaining two-thirds, and the other environmental interests of crofting areas, should be similarly protected.

3.41

Crofters within the current ESA have generally welcomed its designation, with over 60% joining the scheme. The agreements entail a range of measures including retaining rotational cultivation on the machair and not cutting hay or silage before 14 July. In return the crofter is entitled to payments of between £300 and £1000 per croft per annum.

3.42

In *A Future for Environmentally Sensitive Farming*, the RSPB (1991) recommended the following changes to the existing Machair of the Uists and Benbecula, Barra and Vatersay ESA :
- higher payments for corncrake-friendly cutting techniques;
- incentives to revert from summer pasture to hay meadows; and
- encouragement of rotational cultivation.
We would suggest that these changes could be made by incorporating into the ESA scheme additional payments for corncrake-friendly cutting and for each hectare of late-cut silage or hay that is grown (as under the Corncrake Grant Scheme in Northern Ireland) and by reintroducing the Marginal Cropping Grant for other cultivated land.

● **Recommendation 4**

SOAFD should improve the existing Machair of the Uists and Benbecula, Barra and Vatersay ESA, extend ESA agreements to at least 10 years and designate other substantial parts of the crofting counties as Environmentally Sensitive Areas, with the aim that all crofters become eligible for such a scheme.

3.43

As mentioned earlier, fodder conservation is very important in crofting areas. Over recent years there has been a general trend away from hay to silage production. In Scotland, the hay area has fallen by 26% since 1982, while the silage area has more than tripled. There are several reasons for this shift, the main ones being that silage is less weather dependent and so can be cut earlier, is less labour-intensive (especially where hay needs to be dried on fences), and is easier to fit around other jobs. However, silage is less easy to handle and more costly to produce. A recent study (ACLU and Nature Consultants, 1991) estimated that the variable costs of producing a hectare of silage were £155, compared with only £70 per hectare for hay. Even if the cost of hiring contractors for turning and baling is included (approx £50), hay is still cheaper.

3.44

Payments for delaying the cutting of silage or hay until later could be seen as insurance against losses due to poor weather. It would help self-sufficiency, reducing the need for bought-in hay. At the very least, it would probably maintain present levels of hay.

3.45

Similar payments to those in Northern Ireland of £25 per hectare could be offered to crofters for using corncrake-friendly cutting techniques (ACLU and Nature Consultants, 1991) and a further £50 per hectare could be paid for each hectare of silage or hay that is grown, as long as it is cut after 14 July. This latter rate is lower than in Ireland because the usual cutting date in Scotland (25 July for hay) is about 4 weeks later than in Ireland. Such a requirement should not be onerous for crofters.

● **Recommendation 5**

A premium for late-cut silage and hay should be introduced. This could initially be run by SNH as a Corncrake Grant Scheme (similar to that in Northern Ireland), but in the long-term the coordinating agency should manage the premium as part of the overall environmentally sensitive farming scheme.

3.46

The reintroduction of the Marginal Cropping Grant would have at least two beneficial effects. It would encourage the growth of feed for cattle, and hence help to redress the balance between cows and sheep. It should also help to maintain and could enhance the mosaic of land uses. A similar payment to that for growing hay (£50 per hectare) is suggested.

● **Recommendation 6**

The Marginal Cropping Grant should be reintroduced.

3.47

To give an indication of the likely cost of this extension and improvement to the ESA, we need to look at current payment rates and areas. The average size of crofts in the income survey was 21.6 hectares, excluding common grazing. A croft of this size would be entitled to £800 for joining an ESA under the current payment rates and we can assume that only the 9,000 or so active crofters are likely to join. This would bring the total cost of extending the ESA to £7.2 million.

3.48

Additionally, the cost of supporting late-cut grass conservation, assuming that 50% of the area currently cut (28,066 hectares) would take up this option, would be a further £1.1 million. The cost of reintroducing the Marginal Cropping Grant would be £0.6 million, assuming a 100% take up.

3.49

Under a system of cross compliance, joining this new improved ESA would entitle the crofter to receive other support, in the form of livestock hectarage payments and rural development payments.

For an ESA scheme to be successful, it must be integrated with other support. If an ESA works in opposition to the greater incentives for food production under the CAP, the scheme will fail in its objective of protecting the environment. This is why any reform of the CAP must make it less production oriented.

Charles Tait

New support structures should enhance livestock diversity

M W Richards/RSPB

The re-introduction of the Marginal Cropping Grant would benefit corn buntings

Hugh Webster

Well managed grassland is rich in plant life

53

LESS PRODUCTION ORIENTED

3.50

Until recently, virtually all financial support for farming under the CAP has been production related, with the main aims being food production and maintaining farmers' incomes in an effort to keep them farming. The CAP has been overly successful in meeting the first of these aims resulting in surpluses, but has had much less success with the second, with 88,000 farmers giving up farming over the last 10 years in the UK (MAFF, 1991b). In both cases part of the reason for the outcome has been the method of support, in the form of headage and tonnage payments. Part-time and lower intensity systems such as crofting lose out on this form of support, because their output will always be lower than in the relatively favourable agricultural areas of Europe.

3.51

Current support gives no incentive for stock management and therefore encourages stocking at unsustainable levels. The selling price for a cast ewe is sometimes less than the headage payments, especially if the ewe must be transported to the mainland before the sale. Headage payments were up to £18.02 in 1990 and are expected to be £30.81 in 1992. This gives an incentive to keep the ewes for longer.

3.52

The incentive should be for good agricultural practice instead. Paying livestock subsidies by the hectare rather than by the head would go some way towards this. Such a scheme need cost no more in total than the present system, but would change the distribution of the support. The poorer quality land (eg the least productive crofting areas) where the stocking rate is lower would benefit, and much of the incentive to stock at the maximum possible level, regardless of the effect on the quality of the stock, would be removed.

3.53

Currently the average stocking rate in the crofting areas is 0.76 livestock units per adjusted hectare (where a cow accounts for 1 livestock unit and a ewe 0.15, as under EC regulations, and rough grazing is adjusted to its permanent pasture equivalent). This average stocking rate varies considerably between counties, ranging from 0.52 in Ross and Cromarty to 1.83 in Shetland. The total headage payments at the

---

A RETIRED CROFTER in Inverness-shire, no longer working the croft.

Now a widow and tenant of only 1 croft of 2 ha, which a relative uses (unofficially) for extra grazing. 10 years ago she gave up her 9 cows and assigned the other two crofts she used to work, as she no longer felt fit enough to work them. "I wouldn't consider assigning this croft. After I'm gone it will go to a young member of my family who is too young just now, but has an interest in crofting."

"When we were crofting, people made a living of sorts from their produce. We had potatoes, milk and butter, crowdie and eggs. We sometimes had cabbage and turnip too, occasionally peas. Today people don't bother to milk cows, it's cheaper to buy milk and let the calves feed off the cows. People couldn't milk a cow today. But we had 9 cows and calves, and we would keep 1 cow for the house; the other cows had their calves at foot. Calf prices were good for a time, especially after the War, and we had a calf subsidy which helped.

"There is no corncrake today - I haven't heard one for years. There's no cropping any more here. I believe there are plenty of foxes though.

"I think the buying of crofts was the worst thing that ever happened for crofters. Bits and pieces of land are being sold to undesirables. The attraction for richer people from outside is undoubtedly the much cheaper homes which they can avail of here."

moment are £10.5 million for ewes and £5.7 million for cows. On average each adjusted hectare receives £62. If no increase in the total cost is envisaged, the crofter with an average stocking rate of 0.76 would receive the same amount of livestock subsidies as at the moment. A crofter with a lower stocking rate would receive more support than now, and one with a higher rate would receive less support. The latter could continue to receive market returns from the extra animals, or could choose to reduce stocking rates and thus save on input costs and at the same time often improve on the quality of the remaining stock. For administrative ease, the per hectare payment would probably be calculated at a regional level, eg for all of NW Scotland, and the average

stocking rate would probably be higher than 0.76; for all LFA livestock farms in Scotland, it is 1.09 (MAFF, 1991a). Thus, the majority of crofters would benefit.

3.54

We are proposing that this change to hectarage payments be linked through cross compliance to the broader sensitive farming scheme. This should ensure that the move to hectarage payments will not lead to a further increase in stocking levels. Support must no longer be related just to the level of production. We are not suggesting that crofters receive more support for producing less, but that they are entitled to support for a combination of livestock production and the provision of public goods.

● **Recommendation 7**
Livestock subsidies should be converted from a headage to a hectarage basis.

LOCALLY APPROPRIATE

3.55

Given the unique system of crofting, with its particular tenure system and its organisation into townships, any support system should be designed with this in mind. We recommend that conservation plans are drawn up by each township, with information and advice from people outwith the township wherever necessary. These plans would detail the conservation resource of the township and consider how to maintain the balance between the dangers of intensification on the one hand and lack of management on the other.

A GOOD TOWNSHIP in Ross-shire, with 15 active crofters and 2,186 ha of grazings. The total souming (maximum grazing level permitted) is for 123 cows and their followers and 1,074 sheep, but they currently have 12 cows and just over 1,000 sheep.

The main ingredient of a good crofting township is active crofters working within it. Another important thing is that they work together as a community, helping each other with gatherings and when necessary. A good township can play a vital role in developing the local community.

The township shares transport of animals to sale, dipping, clipping, lambing and gathering. There is good consultation over decisions taken and "we meet as and when there is a need". The township management rules are formally confirmed with the Crofters Commission. They deal with the constitution, the souming, procedures for excess stock, the removal and control of stock, payments to herds or shepherds, management of bulls and tups, gatherings of stock, sheep dipping, peat cutting, seaweed, maintenance of fixed assets and muir burning.

Since 1976, grazing land has been taken out of crofting for a refuse tip, a radio mast, a water storage tank, a tourist development and a fish farm. None of the areas were large, and due compensation was received. "The 76 Act isn't all bad in that respect. The owner occupier issue worries me, though. Crofts are going to people with the highest bid, and incomers have moved into every corner. They're not interested or experienced in the ways of a good township."

The local crofters range from 20 to 70 years old. "I consider this a great boost in passing on old and new ways: it's an education for all to have such a wide range of experience. A good community spirit is important. It was created over the generations through need. It's not so necessary today but is still present in most crofting communities. Mercifully."

C H Gomersall/RSPB

Hen harrier

Dennis Coutts

Up-Helly-A, Shetland

Hugh Webster

Loch Torridon, Wester Ross

3.56

Such plans should set appropriate levels of grazing, paying special attention to what is sustainable in the long-term. Consideration should not only be given to the overall level of stocking, but also to the ratio of sheep to cattle, to the seasonal differences in grazing (generally more damage to vegetation occurs during the winter months) and to local problems of overgrazing; for example, where fothering occurs. The powers of grazing committees would need to be strengthened in order to agree and enforce such conservation plans where they relate to common grazings.

3.57

Conservation plans would also indicate how existing woodlands should be managed and which areas and species are appropriate for new tree planting. Only on the areas outlined in the conservation plans would grants for planting and maintenance of woodlands be provided (through the coordinating agency).

3.58

The ESA management agreements could be fine-tuned to make them more appropriate to crofting. A premium could be included for townships that manage their stock communally to the standard laid out in the conservation plan. The plans could also consider whether access by people wishing to visit crofting areas for recreation needs to be managed.

3.59

Additionally, for island crofters, a concession on freight costs could be included in return for joining the sensitive farming scheme. Islanders already receive some preferential rates on the ferries. Vouchers for use on the ferry could be supplied to those crofters signing an ESA-type contract, which the ferry company could then submit to the coordinating agency for reimbursement.

● **Recommendation 8**
Townships should draw up conservation plans, detailing management of grazing, woodlands and access, and in return be entitled to woodland grants, communal management premia and concessions on freight costs.

A LESS SUCCESSFUL TOWNSHIP in Skye and Lochalsh district, with only one active crofter and 24 ha of fenced grazing, 526 ha unfenced hill grazing. The souming is 4 ha per sheep.

The township has the drawbacks of absenteeism, vacant crofts, an ageing population and small unviable holdings. Not many people are active, only 1 out of the 16 crofters keeps stock. There is a lack of commitment. Some of the units are less than 1 ha. Some are poorly laid out, long and thin (eg 14 m by 365 m). Another difficulty is that much of the grazing is unfenced and not nearby. The land is poor, with no shelter. The records have also been poor in the past; when the township grazing was fenced, it transpired that it was less than half the size on record.

The township grazings were fenced a few years ago under the Skye Development Programme. "That was a situation when the township did cooperate and achieve something together. But then, as soon as it was fenced, a crofter from an adjoining township came and put his stock on the ground. He has no official sub-let, but no action has been taken as he has a tacit agreement with relatives who have got a share. As far as I know I am the only one with official sub-lets within the township.

"Livestock production is what has shaped the land here: it is what the whole thing is based on. If you remove that, what is going to come along behind it? Part of the attractiveness of the landscape is the mosaic that agricultural use gives. Diversification is fine, but not everyone can have a scallop unit, a self-catering chalet or move into telecommunications.

"We have everything going for us in green terms. But it's a double edged sword. We have got to recognise that the main purpose of the aid, wherever it comes from, is keeping people on the ground. People are what makes the land and if we lose sight of that fact, we won't do either party a lot of good."

Lower transport costs would help the marketing of crofting produce

and convert their land to woodland or dispose of it by sale or lease for the enlargement of other holdings, though this has not been applied in the UK. A system of direct income aids could be introduced into the crofting areas for paying to inactive, elderly crofters on the condition that they pass on their croft to new, young crofters. This should encourage elderly, less active crofters to decroft their house and garden ground and assign the resulting bareland croft to a suitable young would-be crofter.

● **Recommendation 10**
The UK government should introduce direct income aids for crofters over 55 years old, who are not working their croft and who agree to assign it to a new would-be crofter.

● **Recommendation 9**
Grazing committees should be given the power to enforce these plans where they relate to common grazings.

3.60

Since 1988 Member States have been able to grant early retirement pensions to farmers of 55 years and over who choose to give up farming

A TRADITIONAL CROFTER in Sutherland with a full-time professional job, working 3 crofts, totalling 18.2 ha in-bye land. Grows 5 ha of hay, some turnips and potatoes and keeps 6 cows and 130 breeding ewes.

Over the last 10 years cattle numbers have remained constant, while sheep numbers have gradually increased, from about 50 sheep 10 years ago to 130 now. "Last year was my biggest boost: I held onto sheep because of the poor prices - in 1988 my cast ewes were fetching ú35; in 1990 they were down to ú20."

He earns less from his croft today than ten years ago, mainly because of lower sheep prices. Despite that, "there is the satisfaction of seeing a crop grown from seed; a field of good quality hay - your feed for winter time; the wee lambs and calves growing up. Watching the sun rising; to wake up and hear the birds; the first oystercatcher. Everyone to his own; some would hate to be up at five in the morning. You see the life cycle of plants and animals. It makes you realise just how insignificant you are.

"Conservationists should listen and learn from crofters because there's no substitute for the experience of working and watching the land. And it may be that crofters should pay a wee bit more attention to conservationists. There is more common ground between the two than they can see."

He sees the withdrawal of support as a potential threat to crofting. "Support for crofting has to be seen in the light of support for the community - it's support for a way of life. It's preserved the naturalness of the crofting counties. For too long crofters have been a silent minority."

Figure 3.6

Existing Support System for Crofting
Total £23.5 million in 1990

(CCAGS;   Crofting Counties Agricultural Grants (Scotland) Scheme).

(CBGLS;   Crofters Building Grants and Loans Scheme).

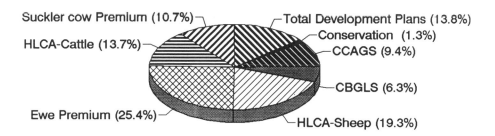

Figure 3.7

New Support System for Crofting
Total £32 million, 1995

(CCAGS;   Crofting Counties Agricultural Grants (Scotland) Scheme).

(CBGLS;   Crofters Building Grants and Loans Scheme).

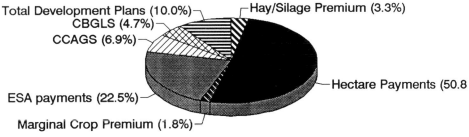

Table 3c

Comparison of net farm income on an "average" croft under the existing and the proposed methods of support

	(Average per holding per annum)	
	1989	1995
Number of beef cows	4	5
Number of ewes	91	80
Total livestock units	17	16
Stocking Density	0.77	0.73
Output (£):		
Crops	167	300
Livestock	4153	3950
Misc	376	1150
Total Output	4697	5400
Total Inputs (£)	4137	4100
Net Farm Income (£)	560	1300

CONCLUSION

3.61

In 1990, the crofting areas received £23.5 million in public support, mostly through the Common Agricultural Policy and through rural development schemes, as shown in figure 3.6. These schemes often contradict the stated objectives of the EC and the UK government that they should benefit the environment and provide incentives to provide public goods. We believe that crofting has always provided society with a whole suite of public goods, from maintaining the culture of crofting and the Gaelic language, to maintaining a rich and varied environment. The authorities have recognised that society should support those who provide such benefits to society, and we have outlined ways in which this can be done.

3.62

Figure 3.7 summarises the support we would like to see going into crofting areas. We estimate that in total this vision would cost around £32 million at today's prices. We believe that such an increase of around 35% is justifiable on the grounds that it would be well targeted, providing the kinds of public goods that society demands. We would expect the payments on ESAs to rise considerably, to £7.2 million. Turning livestock subsidies from headage payments to hectarage payments would cost no more but would result in considerably less pressure from overgrazing. We would hope to see payments under the Marginal Cropping Grant scheme and the late-cutting premium scheme increase over time as the areas under both crops and silage/hay expanded.

● **Recommendation 11**
Financial support for crofting should be increased in recognition of the public goods and services provided by crofters.

3.63

For the individual croft joining the new scheme, we estimate that net farm income would more than double to £1300 (see table 3c). This assumes that an 'average' crofter would enter the environmentally sensitive farming option; becoming entitled to the Marginal Cropping Grant on half a hectare of crops, the premium on one and a half hectares of late cut silage or hay and the hectarage payments on the livestock area. The number of beef cows would increase from 4 to 5, while the number of ewes would fall from 91 to 80, resulting in a slightly lower overall stocking density.

3.64

Integrating all the schemes under one umbrella, using cross compliance, should result in savings in administration costs and should ensure coordination between the various components of the scheme. It would result in a support system that was not only integrated, but less production oriented, more conservation oriented, and more appropriate to crofting.

Charles Tait

Eribol, Sutherland

CHAPTER FOUR
THE WAY FORWARD

4.1

This paper makes the case for a new, and much more positive, approach to crofting. That approach would bring benefits to the wildlife with which crofting has always been associated, to crofting communities and to the rest of the population which has a growing interest in safeguarding and enhancing the outstanding natural environment.

4.2

While a great deal of the detail of future environmental, agricultural and rural policy has still to be settled at both the United Kingdom and the European Community level, the crofting strategy suggested in this paper is one that can certainly be justified in the context of the general objectives already agreed by policy-makers.

4.3

Future policy will give a lower priority to food production. It will give a correspondingly higher priority to environmental considerations and to the need to sustain a comparatively well-populated and economically-diversified countryside. Policy will also set more and more store on the need to maintain distinctive cultures and languages.

4.4

This very basic shift in policy is now occurring. The consequent process of adjustment will not be painless. But that process, this paper maintains, also provides crofting interests with an unprecedented opportunity to make the case for crofting in a way which demonstrates the national and international significance of crofting as a means of enabling rural families to live on the land and earn reasonable livelihoods while simultaneously conserving the natural environment.

4.5

The paper makes various suggestions as to how a better crofting future can be secured. These suggestions do not have to be accepted in detail. They may well be modified - or, in some instances, even rejected and replaced - in the course of the discussion and debate which this paper is intended to initiate.

4.6

On one point, however, the paper's authors are absolutely categorical. It is vital that all of us who are concerned about the future wellbeing of crofting immediately take steps to ensure that Scotland's crofting areas benefit as fully as possible from the new agricultural, rural and environmental policies now being agreed by EC member states. Equally, the conservation of Scotland's outstanding wildlife depends, in part, on a secure future for crofting - supported in a way that gives high priority to environmental objectives.

4.7

This paper can itself be regarded as marking the beginning of that process. The SCU and The RSPB will be drawing the paper strongly to the attention of both the British Government and the European Commission.

4.8

Serious and detailed attention has to be given to reforming crofting support and crofting administration in ways which will permit crofting communities to realise their full potential and to capitalise effectively on the new opportunities now opening up to them. If, as the paper's authors are unanimously convinced, the case for crofting can be made successfully in Edinburgh, London and Brussels, it will quickly become essential to provide policy-makers in these centres with much more detailed information about the implications of the new and improved crofting order which this paper aspires to bring about.

4.9

The paper outlines a number of major changes and modifications in the financial support mechanisms available to crofting. Although some of these may require further exploration, others can be implemented immediately. We urge the relevant organisations to recognise how urgent the need for change is and implement these proposals.

4.10

The paper also suggests that there is a need to simplify and streamline crofting administration. This also merits further exploration.

4.11

Both the SCU and the RSPB will be continuing to examine these issues and to lobby and campaign on behalf of crofting and the Highlands and Islands environment. Both organisations appreciate, however, that progress is more likely to be made if the various agencies dealing directly with crofting support and administration can themselves be persuaded to participate directly in the process of debate, consultation and discussion which this paper is intended to initiate. We look, in particular, to the Scottish Office Agriculture and Fisheries Department, the Crofters Commission, Highlands and Islands Enterprise and Scottish Natural Heritage in this regard. We believe these agencies ought to engage constructively with us, and with each other, in order to help secure the various reforms and improvements which are now becoming attainable.

4.12

Much has been made in the Highlands and Islands in recent years of those disputes and disagreements which have arisen between nature conservation interests, on the one hand, and local communities on the other. Conflict of this type cannot be ruled out in future. But this paper demonstrates that collaboration between crofters and conservationists is also possible. We are convinced that such collaboration is very much in all our interests. We look forward to continuing to work together for a better future for crofting.

Murdo McLeod

REFERENCES

ACLU and Nature Consultants (1991) *Corncrakes and Grassland Management in Britain and Ireland.* Report to RSPB, Sandy.

Arkleton Trust (Research) Ltd (1990) *New Entrants to Crofting.* Report for the HIDB, Inverness.

Batten, LA, Bibby, CJ, Clement, P, Elliot, GD and Porter, RF (1990) *Red Data Birds in Britain.* NCC and RSPB. Poyser, London.

Collar, NJ and Andrew, P (1988) *Birds to Watch. The ICBP World Checklist of Threatened Birds.* ICBP, Cambridge.

Commission of the European Community (1975) *Council Directive on Mountain and Hill Farming and Farming in certain Less Favoured Areas.* COM 75/268. CEC, Brussels.

Commission of the European Community (1988) *The Future of Rural Society.* COM 88/2052. CEC, Brussels.

Commission of the European Community (1991a) *The Development and Future of the Common Agricultural Policy.* COM 91/258. CEC, Brussels.

Commission of the European Community (1991b) *Measures to Accompany the Reform of the Market Support Mechanisms.* COM 91/415. CEC, Brussels.

Currie, A (1991) *Crofting in the Hebrides.* In Curtis, DJ, Bignal, EM and Curtis, MA (eds) *Proceedings of the second European Forum on Birds and Pastoralism.* JNCC, Peterborough.

DAFS *Agriculture in Scotland, Annual Reports.* HMSO.

Darling, F Fraser (1955) *Summary of the West Highland Survey: An Essay in Human Ecology,* Oxford University Press, Oxford.

Hunter, J (1991) *The Claim of Crofting.* Mainstream, Edinburgh.

Kinloch, M and Dalton, G (1990) *A Survey of Crofting Incomes - 1989,* Scottish Crofters Union, Skye.

MAFF (1991a) *Farm Incomes in the United Kingdom.* HMSO.

MAFF (1991b) *Agriculture in the United Kingdom: 1990.* HMSO.

MAFF (1991c) *Our Farming Future.* HMSO.

MAFF (1992) *Agriculture in the United Kingdom: 1991.* HMSO.

Revell, BJ, Johns, PM and Kinnair, L (1987) *An Assessment of the Livestock and Meat Industry in the Highlands and Islands - A Statistical Study.* Prepared for HIDB by the North of Scotland Agricultural College, Aberdeen.

RSPB (1991) *A Future for Environmentally Sensitive Farming.* RSPB, Sandy.

Seymour, C (1991) *Review of Environmentally Sensitive Areas in Scotland.* Unpublished report, RSPB, Edinburgh.

Taylor, JP and Dixon, JB (1990) *Agriculture and the Environment: Towards Integration.* RSPB, Sandy.

The Crofters Commission, *Annual Reports,* HMSO

The Crofters Commission (1991) *Crofting in the '90s.* Acair, Stornoway.

UK Agriculture Departments (1991) *Environmental Aspects of Support for Hill Farming.* HMSO.